the under story

New Women's Voices Series, No. 179

poems by

Broderick Eaton

Finishing Line Press
Georgetown, Kentucky

the under story

New Women's Voices Series, No. 179

for Meg

ACKNOWLEDGMENTS

"looking down at the sky" was a finalist for the Slippery Elm prize and
appeared in the 2022 *Slippery Elm* journal.

"unnamed" was a finalist for *Crosswinds Poetry Journal*'s annual contest and
appeared in the 2022 journal.

"the salt we leave behind" was a finalist for *Crosswinds Poetry Journal*'s
annual contest and appeared in the 2023 journal.

"raspberries" received honorable mention in the 2022 New Millennium
contest and was accepted by *Poetry International*'s web publication.

Publisher: Leah Huete de Maines
Editor: Christen Kincaid
Cover Art: Broderick Eaton
Author Photo: Nathaniel Eaton
Cover Design: Elizabeth Maines McCleavy

Order online: www.finishinglinepress.com
also available on amazon.com

Author inquiries and mail orders:
Finishing Line Press
PO Box 1626
Georgetown, Kentucky 40324
USA

Contents

in the time of trees

slant light standoff sun to moon
sawtooth horizon grows sharper
dying sky cut to simmering shreds
on treetops aiming for the night
the long hem of summer day
unthreads burning into deep blue
as falling darkness fills river with stars

somewhere in the marriage of it all
a quiet violence as night overcomes
light yet tomorrow the day returns new
over and again or is this imagined
does time have no care for moment or need
will the stars flood in and the river shine
the mountains pine and the trees rock
forever as they hold together underground

the light will surge again and subside
once more everything swallowed by cycle
made invisible soon enough sometimes too
soon disappeared with the gone mountains
slipped into the pinpointed slick of the river
lost in the dark with trees whose needles
never leave and whose leaves grow back
they have seen the coming the going
standing firm in the night   resting
waiting to embrace the light

(unnamed)

ask me my name and I might tell you
to turn toward the leaves
listen to their husk and mumble
stand over the plunge of the river
lose yourself in the slick fear
crawling down your limbs or pull
at the throaty sounds hulled between stone
and root under a log that once stood
straight and mighty sweeping the sky
hear the hush and push of lifting wing
the vanishing miracle of flight
carved by an arrow of starlings
find a word for filtered light
sifting through capillaried petals
capture the sound of unsettled wind
carding the sinews of dried grasses
try to describe the way darkness curves
its somber path around the moon—

whatever you call the least of these
this is what you may call me too

raspberries

bright flowers burst
across my tongue and deep
in my childhood
grandfather bends
over lush summer bushes
his basket nearly full

he will stand with a groan
place a hand on the small
of his back and point
to a twinkling sphere
that tumbles across the blue
miles above the garden

now what do you suppose that is
he will ask as he turns for the house
where grandmother waits with pie crust
but I stay to watch the orb disappear
I never knew if he meant the pain
in his back or the flashing craft in the sky

he wouldn't be on this earth much longer
and when I'm nearly the age
grandfather was that day my mother
will tell me those were his worry words
that's what his panic sounded like
we both wonder what crossed the heavens

I still don't know how to name
all the miracles that form a life
but I can recognize the gift
of moment and the awe found in sun
water and soil even the soft give of flesh
another berry staining my fingers

after the fire

every warm season
waving lodgepole mothers
drop cone clusters
with no hope of ever
seeing their babies
but their faith
seeds the earth
and waits

hidden deep in rich loam
perfect for their needs
the kernels sleep and sleep
for years stacked into decades
ignoring sun and rain until
finally one lightning day
the devastation of fire
takes their mothers away
burns the elders' needles
their bark and cambium
to blackened trunk and ash

but there—
what ruins the surface
summons seedlings
hard shells burst by trial
they break through new
a supple release from loss
thin skin shoots reach
and reach to greet the air
to feel the rain run down
feathered stalks and they rise
and rise next to the bodies
of their kin

to open and grow
from scorched self
remember this lesson

nurse log
for the trees who invited mary oliver in

from studies done in the language of humans
scientists think only trees or other inanimates
with leaves drink the sun and pull nourishment
from deep soil   hold hands in the dirt   feel life
surge from above and below at once but they didn't
understand the language sung to them

a young one awoke every early morning
as if sustained by wild and precious possibility
just as the sun wiped sleep from shine eyes
she was already in the woods walking
her silent communion among fellow beings
waiting in awe for the invisible dream

raised by broad shoulders of grandmother oak
veined maple hands and flowering dogwood
she learned to speak with pine and fir
to clap in abundance with aspen's toss
accept gifts of branch   regrowth   and air
bare feet rooted in these soiled promises

she knew with enough patience and wonder
the divine light would fall to find her
each day a gift to be opened slowly
alone and without words for no tamed sound
can measure how it feels to be held in arms
extended through time without question or reserve

old oak is long gone and maybe many others
she knew fell to age or disease or worse
her gifts now scattered to the wind   her words
borne on a breeze past clapping stands
of poplar and birch eyeing the next listener
she knew from the trees the streams the falling sky

love is something that must be shared
even if simply given without return
perhaps that love sewn into a place
tethers a soul in space and time
so it can return to visit what was left
maybe this is what is meant by heaven

maybe she knew this and is still there
in the rustle of leaves or in the gentling
brush of needle against trunk or the push
of wind moving pollen into the future
never demanding but urgent *tell me*
she whispers through the dancing light
what is it you plan to do

when the trees

speak they do not wander into extremes
they do not blame the sun for sinking
leaving us in darkness   maybe they know
there is no time and we are the ones who turn

away only to return the following day   again
and again the leaves sing a hymn of thanks
as light drops through and through their skin
borrowing their hues to share with the air

would you believe me if I told you
we all belong to the light   our bodies
every tree and its leaves   we stole ourselves
away from stardust falling through space

long ago to land and grow and gather the colors
until we learn to hold all that we are given
in lush and breathing bunches the cresting
of life over the resting shadows

it seems only right   then   when the sun
grows distant and the trees pull back
their sap each leaf   completed   sails alone
on its own path into the grace of flight

felling

i.
two willows at water's
edge   limbs entwined
twinned from season
after season together
each knows the other's
most intimate curve
most private dimple
most secret fear
of falling
in winter breeze embraced
they brush each other
with early buds that grow
now on only one

ii.
what does a tree do
when one rooted with it
is cleaved from this life and
collapses into the river?
they have been one
for so long now
their moss   their leaves
their matching rings
have grown together so
you can no longer tell
where one ends and
the other begins
the one   sickened and weak
groans as he leans
on his kin and tilts away
snapping branches that held him
arms grown from the same root
left torn and weeping on the shore

september river

old crow laughs low
dragging his shadow down the river
where two willows twinned
from the same trunk anchored
deep beneath the riverbank
send serpents of root rising through soil
as they lean across the water
caress the current with green fingers
tinged in orange tasting
the fleeting history of snow
the slow cataclysm of falling
the inevitable pull of ashes and ocean

birdwatching

after a bout of rare cancer
my friend became convinced
that birds determine his existence
and as he rebalances among the familiar
remains he searches for life above

each morning he rises into the light
before coffee before the news
and looks from the window
to find the bird that confirms his own
renewed flight across this land

today he awoke again just like
yesterday in another tomorrow
this one the same tomorrow as his
dream where his children fledge
and begin to learn their own wings

his wife of all those years stands
next to him seeking what he needs
so close that even without touching
they carry a tenacious nest of warmth
between their proximate hands

the part of me made of sky and feather
somewhere in my coding understands
a need to find meaning in each new day
to look for fellow flyers even the pull
to tether one warm being to another

I gave this friend a small carved bird
made of wood chipped into the form
of a robin with its head tilted one eye
aimed at the earth the other scanning
for what might come out of the blue

now every morning the two can search
for birds outside the window and the time
no wing slides its shadow over the pane
they will turn their ticking flush hearts to find
they already have what they thought was lost

to the waiting tilth

through the open window tolling   tolling
church bells peal into the heavens   not
for the hour or its half   or even a quarter
solemn clang   marking instead a moment
outside of time   a revelation to every ear
the declaration of loss

under the weight of such herald   I pause
to sit and eye   signs of life now passed
a demilune on paper   from yesterday's coffee
the empty box on a shelf   bearing the last thing
my father wrote   and that's why
I can't throw it out

on the table a cunning star   in the center
of a tangerine peel   whose perfect button
once held the curve of pocked skin   no longer
whole and I think   of my grandmother
her hand an autumn leaf   curled
in the soft cradle of my own

and the bells   the bells   the blessed bells
what does time mean   how does this construct
dictate the passing   of anything
the earth opens its womb   in answer
through the same window   the fresh scent
of new-turned tillage

front porch ambedo

eyesome and full
this pummeled spring
drawn from tired winter
sudden hailstones abating
now the memory tide of nothing
hits the ear with a roar and
I am reminded how much
can be heard in silence

crimson weeping of poppies
their spent petals plastered
to the soiled riches at their feet
scattered lifeless on the walk
their exposed stalks shorn free
whipping naked and obscene

there in the garden glinting from a shaft
of gold a mudded toy car turned up
under my shovel its long ago
allure muted by time and weather
by roots of things I've planted
there is the quick dagger—my boys
don't play with small cars anymore

but is that bright toy even real
were those poppies truly crimson
I have been told that I am deceived
somehow what I see is not seen
that color does not exist
it is merely a construct of the mind

I will watch the grayscale sky
until atmospheric wind pulls clouds
stretches them apart like ribbon candy
mirroring my thoughts carded
over the bones of recollection
the quicksilver days gone so soon

maybe cobwebs gather in the corners
to keep the last of everything

from drifting away

looking down at the sky

beneath our feet I peer
at an upside-down world
reflected in the puddled Portland sidewalk
I avoid stepping on clouds out of reverence
or maybe fear of falling through
that alternate sky and leaving my family
in a cold that settles quickly over concrete
and the path grows stippled with snow

the warm building draws us inside out
of our coats and gloves and we feel
a little more than we feel like feeling
having just learned of the death
of a loved one on Christmas day
her shell discovered only hours ago
next to her phone with the unsent text
didn't we have fun!

numb from this news or the cold
we adjust our masks and pass
through the line and into a darkened room
where empty frames hang between canvases
and together we fall into a world transformed
by paint and self-loathing and the determined love
between the Van Gogh brothers—their letters
and patterns of color all that remains

somber silence seems appropriate
for this moment as we wander
and read and hug our coats each of us
on our own journey through this exhibit
where I look up and see my husband
his brother and aunt and each of my sons
individually captured in gilded frames
their profiles distilled   suddenly more profound

the final room is self-portraits and paintings
of others Vincent knew projected onto every wall
even the floor where I sit because I grow dizzy
        there is the sky under me again falling apart in a blizzard
of spring petals swirling over the images
before bouquets bloom across   the vanishing faces
        every face disappears   to become flowers   and oh—
                                    aren't they glorious

of life

and the tree
trades needle for shadow
threaded sharp against
the pinking sky

and the eve
now blues against blues
shifts the eye
from day into dark

and the tree
there but no longer
its memory the unnaming
of things I once knew

and you and me and you
did we lose shape of us
when we couldn't see
each other anymore

and the tree
silent yet never still
and still there if unseen
roots the branches here

and the being
the miracle of being
begins it all
the coming   the going

you   me
    the tree

one hundred winds

the wind comes a hundred
different ways with a hundred
different motives but who is counting
each time it gently presses pale stems
into strength or flays its rage into the arms
of the ancient trunk whose roots tremble
grasp at the soil but cannot weather
this last

as cool moves in, the long hot breath
of a distant sun carries off the old
the dry   the forgotten   everything
no longer tethered by sinew and thought

is the wind jealous   can it envy
our stability or does it slap our walls
comb urgent fingers through our hair
raising bumps on the skin and the pines
and cottonwoods become stolen memory
after coveted scent is cajoled from slender
branches that bend to its whim
where does the tart sap smell land
does it disappear or change to blend in
to this new land this unfamiliar geography

there's really nothing that can stay
if a stronger force has other ideas
I learned once as I stepped off
a mountaintop formed when the mother
beneath us poured her seething insides into stone
that you don't hear the wind anymore
when you let go   and fly

what if I told you

I can't remember the language
I once shared with the wind
this silence is not golden
as I've been told
now I wait   mute and hoping
the wind will recognize me again
or
long ago I had a dream
I tore open the summer sky
to let the stars pour through
because I forgot how to trust
they were still there
then I had all the stars in my hands
and could not put them back
and the night   oh
the night was so dark
but
sometimes I have to pry my eye
from staring into the sun
even though I know
I know this could be the last
thing I look at
and would it be so bad
to drift into obscurity
from such impossible brightness
yet
always this saline tide
pushed by hearts broken over and over
through my veins and yours
as though we share the same blood
I suppose we do
if you look back
long enough
then

I wonder if you can feel
the wild rising   that skipped beat
in your chest   the thing you can't control
as it sends you forward
through the darkness the wind
even the fallen stars
held as sparks in your eyes
until they too give in   flicker out
and our words fly away
following the wind

november

between voluptuous mountain folds
sharpened blue by frost
a deep pool hushes
reins back
on the bridle of the stream
stay a longer while
and listen to the trees

falling
leaves but a memory
come the winter absence   empty
there   where stream freezes in place
firs bristle and brace tight
fisted boughs against the coming cold
mountain aspens clatter
red and yellow shingles   so quick
to shed at first wind of snow
chilled fingers   clap their dry coins
                                        and release

springsong

deep in the fleet creek
cunning fish paint with light
until they are no longer visible
in a lazy flow that grows
from the quickening spring
an awakening beneath frosted soil
heaves its breast toward a world
where birdsong rests on air waiting
for new ears to come near

my vivisected pieces
I carry around the whole
parted by loss   by years
I bring them into the trees
set them at the feet of winter
think about the theory of birds
their return after they've flown
the vanishing of snow
the flight of a single sparrow
alight then winging and gone

what wonder to let things go
to watch the stream slip away
limited by what the eye can see
held between tree and cloud
breathless
as I wait for the answer
an arrow of birds breaks
sky silence and my heart
follows aloft

songbird

send your feet down
the silent path to merge
the hollow with shadow
      embrace the wholeness
      of nothing
as you draw the trees deep through
your eyes into your heart your
memory your broken
bond with the stillness
      the living and breathing
      trees won't talk
      in a way you can hear
      but still you
must listen see interpret
what the emptiness holds
between the trunks like pillars
holding up the light   there—
time is now a staircase
built of words you cannot say
      leaf litter night fall feel
      the shape of loss sifted
fingers deep in the mud that roots you
filter an unconscious tune
sent through a hidden songbird
leading you out of the woods
      to see the light
of a single star

this is a pilfered poem

from deep shadowed woods
ponderosa juniper bitterbrush
shifted into silhouette
before coral fire setting sun
the coming velvet nape of night and oh—
the impossible spray of stars

here is where I admit I've stolen

pleasure from the sacred rhythm
of spring's first innocent rain
tap-tapping the earth awake
          I even used the shine of my eyes
to devour the vision of an early flower
bursting at my feet just now

I've derived more than my portion

of breath caught in the throat
from new powder peaks when
clouds sweep open after the storm
          of lungs heaved deep to consume
freshets of spring into this body thriving
on whatever clarity the air might share

but I've never forgotten

how the silvered moon relies on the sun
for its full face to be seen   for me
to believe it's still there in the night
          that the pinecone showed
after falling and falling and shattering
the pieces find footing to root and rise

I prefer to think I borrowed

these sights   this life without

the weighted ghost of owning it all
but what do I possibly have to offer
in exchange for the dream of being
in return for my self taking flight
into the peached eve of this night

the deep swift

and if along the way
my lips unclean
from a prayer I recall
I came from this river
fledged wet and forged hard
from this same slick body
long before I learned
the difference between
gods and men
between miracles and lies
long before I rose
from my knees and wiped
their faith from my eyes

in the ebbing flow maybe
I pause and remember
to the current I'll return
one day my flesh forgotten
no longer a stranger
to myself

but does a heart
have to break
to be open

under the rebirthed truth
there—new leaves wave
as they grow
into their intended shape
they bend to lap the quiet surface
touching the deep pull
of ashes and ocean
the morning sun bleeding
scarlet through poppies
run wild and the same tide
pushing through the dark
tunnels of my own body

when at last I rest
will I need to wash this life
from my hands or will the river
take me softly into its shape
for I am nothing more than
an echo of what came before

apostate

I am no longer
governed by gods

no—

called to look up
by a dance of early light
buttering the highest reach
of the old oak's technicolor dream
rustling umber over everblack trunk
the leaves still left fall and fall
onto a land gone roan with change

I am not weighed down
by ghosts anymore
maybe now I am lightning's child
or a stone thrombosis forcing quiet
change under the still of the river
baptized by my fall and fall
from the virgin mountain of my birth
to land in the liquid memory of snow

on a low branch the holy trinity
of sky   sun   and water
stop time to form a miracle
the glint of an icicle dagger dropping
every color the eye can absorb
pointing at the earth where it will
eventually give up its grip
then fall and fall to land
a premonition of my own
breathtaking end

but soon—

paper wings
a crocus white as yesterday's snow

will push life into sight
having died and slept
to rise again

renku: pieces

but I created you
said the tumbling stone
cleaved from the mountain

we stand in place shifting
each other from grace

once long ago I let the stars
settle around my eyes
too close to see

I learned that what broke
my heart did not also break yours

landing again I realized
the different shades
of darkness

shadows plucked from heartflesh
now centered here in my hand

warm demand of morning sun
red through eyeskin light presses
into the canyons and sends me rising

rising into the bell of this day
will I toll or will I ring

the salt we leave behind

day has broken
up with me again
first it sharpened
all of its sparrows then
sent them harpooning
into the trees seeking
refuge in branch and flock

noble the day fought
to stay relevant before
dropping golden crown
into the fire of its own
late light and pressing
the coin moon up
from its far bed

I forget what I've cried
over where I've left
my blood in this world
or even why in the quiet
meditation of cooling skin
meeting air I am no stranger
to this saline dream

fluent in silence I watch
the overbloom of stars
take up the day's story
to my eye no shape can hold
itself wrapped in darkness
all of us lost and found
in this neverwhere home

the silk balloon of my heart
the indigo slack of my thoughts
all the rancorous delights
of placing my feet here so long
maybe what I've dropped what

I've left can stay forever woven
into the tapestry of season and kin

this is the lie I tell myself

a year in relief

tightly wrapped buds wait sleeping
deep under crystalline blankets unaware
of their power to pull cellulose beings
and slumbering parts from the long night to spring
unfurled when sun seeks sap and tells it run   now

leaves spread lush rustle and hush
devour the sun as it presses time from their veins
reminding us to touch the light before shadows grow long
to love bright open with our eyes   our hands
our hot lumbering hearts

flat rusting skeletons of what we once knew
spin in the wind before they think of letting go
first trusting the glory of their change
releasing ochre skins   their battered bodies' finest
in the setting fire's dying light

gnarled arthritic limbs reach wildly to the sky
pushing their last into sleeping buds toward a sun
that left them but calls from a distance   promising
redemption when the winter thin shards of our castle
splinter among our kin

long winter

yet the walking onions
send up green periscopes
and the crunch underfoot
as I walk across last year's
grass now cushioned in sprouts
still too short to overtake

the long cold trimmed
the sails of my memory so
I could be surprised again
and again the creek is fluid
running over its banks
with winter gone to water
now the mirrored sky runs
the banks as if to remind me
it is still there even when
I am not looking

but all this time I remember
time has a way of away-ing
dissolving with the hymn of sun
falling through leaves and taking
the color along on its skin
sinking and sinking and making
way for the new honeyed moon

I once thought that time was woven
just for me but I have learned through
the cold the dark   the stunted waiting
that instead I am the one woven into time
tied to the beginning and the rest

I can only go forward but still
start over just as the calendar
bites its own tail and begins again
not at zero   the sum of nothing
but with one   the same number

I come up with on my own

now in winter I look for the buds
no longer needing to know
how will it end
how will it end
how will it end

Broderick Eaton grew up exploring the natural world out her back door in the foothills of the Cascades. She returned permanently to the Pacific Northwest after living in Costa Rica, Virginia, and Spain. As a student at Sweet Briar College, her writing career began when she stumbled into a life-changing introduction to poet Mary Oliver. This turned into informal poetry classes and then independent studies with both Mary Oliver and with author John Gregory Brown. After college, she fell into her first adult iteration as a high school Spanish teacher and completely forgot about writing. Many years later, the muses returned and demanded an audience, and the seeds sewn in that tiny office at Sweet Briar suddenly burst into bloom.

Writing actively for only the last few years, Eaton strives to draw parallel the inexorable rhythms of the natural environment we inhabit and the treasures to be found if only we look around us and live in the moment, in this world full of awe.

After the recent completion of an MFA in Writing from Lindenwood University, Eaton has revisited her interest in fiction and essay and has expanded her repertoire and publication list. Her work has appeared in journals and anthologies such as *Crosswinds Poetry Journal, Slippery Elm, Smartish Pace,* and *Clackamas Literary Review.*

Fluent in English, Spanish, and Italian, she enjoys traveling to far off places, but Central Oregon will always be home. She spends as much time as possible with her family in the forests and mountains of the Pacific Northwest.

www.ingramcontent.com/pod-product-compliance
Lightning Source LLC
Chambersburg PA
CBHW020222090426
42734CB00008B/1187